photo Faber and Faber

P. H. NEWBY

P. H. NEWBY

by

G. S. FRASER

Edited by Ian Scott-Kilvert

PUBLISHED FOR
THE BRITISH COUNCIL
BY LONGMAN GROUP LTD

LONGMAN GROUP LTD
Longman House, Burnt Mill, Harlow, Essex

Associated companies, branches and
representatives throughout the world

First published 1974

Printed in Scotland by
Her Majesty's Stationery Office at HMSO Press, Edinburgh

ISBN 0 582 01237 6

CONTENTS

P. H. NEWBY

CAREER, REPUTATION, IDEAS ON THE NOVEL

PERCY HOWARD NEWBY was born in 1918 at Crowborough, went to Hanley Grammar School, and then trained to be a teacher at St Paul's College of Education, and did a short period of teaching before World War II. He belongs, that is to say, neither to the gentry nor the workers but to the educated middle classes. He served in France in 1939 and was immediately posted to Egypt. In 1942, he was seconded from the army to become a lecturer in English at Fouad Awal University in Cairo. He remained there till 1946, having published his first novel in 1945. He is not an autobiographical novelist, but he does not waste material. He has made use, for instance, of his training college days in *A Step to Silence*, his war experience in *The Retreat*, early teaching in *Mariner Dances*, university teaching in Egypt in *A Season in England* and *The Picnic at Sakkara*. His first two very romantic novels, *Journey to the Interior* and *Agents and Witnesses*, are set in imaginary countries which are obviously fantasized versions of Egypt. In *The Picnic at Sakkara*, *Revolution and Roses*, *A Guest and His Going* and one of his fairly recent novels, *Something to Answer For*, he uses his knowledge of Egypt realistically and directly.

Yet it would be wrong to think of Newby as primarily a novelist of the exotic, like Lawrence Durrell. Most of his novels have English settings, in which, moreover, he is more at home in the small country town than in London. His most recent novel, *A Lot to Ask*, is the only one with a mainly metropolitan setting. His characters belong on the whole to the middle station of life, from education officers, teachers, and doctors in a small way of practice, to bakers, small farmers and lorry drivers. He never takes us inside a factory or to a really smart party. He depicts a slightly old-fashioned, semi-rural England, in which the sense of community is, on the whole, much more important than class distinctions or individual ambition. But he is not a comfortable novelist. Inside his apparently rather cosy settings, he has a masterly gift for evoking tension, suspicion, misunderstanding, and discontent.

We live in an age in which some of our best novelists are satirically and critically preoccupied with the themes both of social injustice and social pretension and with the idea of the man or woman who 'drops out' of society. These are themes which simply do not interest Newby: though he is interested in the psychological, not social, theme of the natural outcast. It would be a rough and ready way of distinguishing him from his contemporaries to say that in nearly all his novels there is some important character who is mad, or on the verge of madness. It should be noticed also that, unlike his near contemporary, Iris Murdoch, he does not write philosophical novels, nor is he interested in the comedy of ideas. He can depict intelligent characters, but they are not more interesting to him than slower or more obtuse characters; he does not write about artists or intellectuals. He is a master of comedy, but it is sympathetic not satirical comedy. In all these ways, he is unfashionable; unfashionable also in a kind of undogmatic religiousness. He does not want to condemn anyone but feels we all have 'something to answer for'. To be alive is to be in a position of immense privilege but it is also to be poised, tottering, on the edge of a precipice. Punishment is something we may deliberately have to seek out.

There are, therefore, many current interests which Newby does not share and many of his personal interests which few people share with him. His talent has had recognition. Early and late in his career he has received, for what such awards are worth, an Atlantic Award, a Somerset Maugham Award, and the recently founded Booker Prize. He is always respectfully reviewed. Yet he seems to exist somewhere on the margin of critical attention, and treatment of him in books on the contemporary novel tends to be polite but perfunctory. His sheer productiveness, which has included a boy's adventure story, a study of Maria Edgeworth, and a good selection from Burton's version of the *Arabian Nights*, may have put critics off. So may his second very successful career in a field very different from that of fiction—sound broadcasting.

Newby left Egypt in 1946 and devoted himself entirely to writing till 1949. He then, less for the sake of money than to renew and enlarge his human contacts, and to learn new skills, joined the staff of the BBC Talks Department and as a talks producer was particularly concerned with the Third Programme, of which he became controller in 1958. My own slight acquaintance with him dates from the early 1950s. I did a lot of Third Programme broadcasting in the 1950s, but it was Newby who started me off by teaching me how to write a script—'You must think in speech blocks, not in paragraphs or sentences'—, how to modulate my voice, and how to address the microphone (as if it were an intimate friend, not a public meeting).

The personal impression Newby made on me on this and subsequent BBC meetings throws some light on the quality of his novels. As might be expected from the editor of Burton's *Arabian Nights* and the biographer of Maria Edgeworth, he gives a double impression of unshockability and primness. One might guess that he had been a teacher, and a good one. He puts one at one's ease but preserves a benign distance. He is quietly formidable, understanding one a great deal better than one understands him, but not frighteningly. But he is not, I would guess, a man for London literary convivialities. He has a house in Buckinghamshire and he keeps his double career going by making a rule of getting away from London as soon as his work is over. I imagine that, like some of his heroes, he is a man whom many people, including comparative strangers, instinctively confide in, but who has perhaps few intimate friends.

After the Pilkington Report on Broadcasting published in the early 1960s, the old Third, Home and Light Programmes were abolished. They suggested too much the old Platonic idea of a tripartite division of society (and of the soul): thinkers, executives, hands: highbrows, middlebrows, lowbrows. It was felt that in a democratic society, even if these separations of taste and social function could not be abolished immediately, at least our awareness of them could be blurred. Newby, whose career in the Third Programme had been very distinguished, may have felt some regrets. He became head of Radio 3, which inherited much of the serious literary and musical content of the Third Programme but without the air of projecting itself, exclusively and excludingly, towards a minority culture. Newby's new role must have been even more arduous than his old, but there was no falling off either in the quantity or in the quality of his writing.

In 1960, when I had recently become a lecturer at Leicester University, Newby accepted my invitation to give a lecture on his ideas about the novel. He was one of half a dozen novelists invited to speak to us in successive weeks. It says something about his character that he was the only one of the six to write a proper script for us: the others improvised, read essays already published, or gave us sample passages from their forthcoming books. Newby is both conscientious and modest. His paper was as much about the novel in general as about his own novels. I am quoting and summarizing with his permission: it is typical again that he never bothered to get a distinguished and interesting essay published.

Newby postulated five demands which he makes, not necessarily of all novels, but no doubt of the novels he finds most sympathetic, and certainly of the novels he writes himself. Firstly, the novel 'particularizes. It breaks down general statements about society and behaviour into the specific and the actual—it confers "a local habitation and a name". . . The novelist says to the moralist and the philosopher, "It's all very well for you to say people *should* behave in such-and-such a way, but I am trying to show you how people in fact do behave".'

Secondly, the novelist should be charitable. Newby here quotes Dostoevsky: 'Consider what it is to be human, consider how you—dear reader!—might have behaved under different circumstances, under different stars.' (I have noted already that Newby's comedy is always sympathetic; he is temperamentally incapable of writing corrective comedy, or satire. It is his most likeable characters, like Edgar Perry and Muawiya in *The Picnic at Sakkara* and *A Guest and His Going*, who often tumble into the most absurd predicaments or do the most foolish things. And he can sympathize with rogues as well as fools. God, so to say, made them that way.)

Thirdly (and here one is reminded of Hardy's belief that the characters and background of a novel should be like life, but the incidents more exciting than life). Newby says: 'The novel deals with the unusual and surprising rather than the matter-of-fact and ordinary.' This is his most controversial contention, and clearly it will not do for the novel in general. It excludes Jane Austen's *Emma*, nearly all Trollope, and Arnold Bennett's *The Old Wives' Tale*. But the contention is true of Newby's own novels, whose plots I have described as essentially romantic. Indeed, one reason why one might hesitate to call Newby a major novelist is that there seems to be a point in all the novels, I would say about two-thirds of the way through, when characters cease to change and develop on their own account and become puppets manipulated by Newby, whose chief concern has suddenly become the plot as such, with its surprises and paradoxes.

Newby's fourth point has some connexion with what I have called his 'undogmatic religiousness', his concern with life's mysterious uncanniness. The novel presents us with 'a situation which seems open to explanation from one point of view and is then seen to require more profound explanation'. The good novelist, in other words, presents us not only with an accurate picture of the surface of life but makes us aware of the cracks in the surface, and of the fact that we never fully understand either our own behaviour or that of other people. This is one of Newby's greatest gifts and a reason perhaps for reconsidering our decision that his habit of letting the plot, at some stage, take mechanical control shuts him out of the ranks of properly major novelists. Newby's novels are as tightly plotted as a good detective story, or a good farce, as Agatha Christie or P. G. Wodehouse, but, unlike the very best of detective stories and farces, they are three-dimensional in their treatment of character, their surprises are often those of life rather than of fictional convention, and they are morally open-ended.

Newby's fifth point about the novel, his most abstract and general and therefore his most theoretically interesting point, is that the form of the novel is retrospective. Everything must have happened before anything can be related. This *is*, of course, the main formal difference between the novel and the lyric poem, which is a timeless or aesthetic equivalent for the *immediacy* of emotion; and between the novel and the drama, which enacts its events—and compared to the events of the novel, they are highly schematized events—in an imaginary suspended present. But in the novel everything has ended as event before anything as narration can begin. This retrospectiveness is one of the unique resources of the novelist, as compared with other kinds of literary artist. It enables him to 'to play off past against present', in a way that poems and plays cannot do. Newby instances how, in *David Copperfield*, the mature David is able to recreate the experiences of the child David with words which the boy would not have had at his command. Thus, also, the re-collected immediacy of the boy David's delights and agonies creates for the mature David in the later stages of the novel, (where the man David is more or less the stock hero of a success story), a sympathy which he would not otherwise elicit.

In this important unpublished essay there are some other interesting general points. One of the most widely discussed topics in novel criticism today is that of 'authorial authority'. 'Never trust the teller, trust the story,' said D. H. Lawrence, though very few great modern novelists have been so ready to interrupt the story in order to tell the reader what he should feel or think. The main questions about authorial authority are these: how does the author know what is happening inside his characters (how do *we* know what is happening inside our friends?): how are we to feel confident in the correctness of the author's judgement about his characters (would we feel confident in the correctness of his judgement about *us*?): what *right* has he to judge? Newby does not answer these questions but like a very deft fencer parries them with a purely technical, but unanswerable, argument: 'Narrative style is that quality in a novel of which the characters could *not* be conscious'.

Newby's most self-revealing remark is about his five years in Egypt:

For the first time, I was living not only outside Europe but outside Christendom, outside a way of life that was still based, even if unconsciously, upon certain Christian beliefs. I suppose this experience is central to me and to my writing. Even when I am not writing about Egypt itself I am pretty sure there is some Egyptian quality about the way I handle English scenes and characters. I learned very much more from my Egyptian students than they learned from me. I learned, I think, some candour and a little of their sense of humour.

For all that, Newby thinks that too much fuss is made about 'national character'. It is our basic common humanity that matters. Shakespeare's ancient Greeks and Romans are Englishmen in fancy dress and none the worse for that.

Finally, at the end of his lecture, Newby admits that he is a 'conventional' novelist. But so is everybody. Sartre's way of doing fiction is

as big a convention as the story Chekov mentioned in connexion with the theatre: if you see a gun on the wall in the first act, you can be sure it will go off in the third. I don't mind this. In fact, I rather like it, it means that the evening's entertainment has been worked out by some rational creature.

It is by that criterion that I shall try to assess Newby's novels, but not only by that criterion. I shall also bear in mind a more profound remark which Newby makes almost as an afterthought, or as if in passing. A satisfactory novel is

so *commanding* that it makes you return and submit again with more questions in your head than there were before you read the book the first time. If it is a good book they will be questions about yourself.

One of the reasons why Newby is important is that he does set one, like an examiner, questions about oneself. The most distinguished English novelist to come into notice about the same time as Newby, around the late 1940s, is Angus Wilson. Wilson is slightly Newby's senior in years, and his earliest work was published a little earlier, but his successful professional career, first at the British Museum and now as a part-time University Professor, might be compared to Newby's as a lecturer in Egypt and an administrator at the BBC. Wilson is a more obviously newsworthy writer, a master of satirical caricature, of bright colours and the broad brush, where Newby is a master of the delicate line and of accurate sympathetic comedy. But Wilson is not very interested in people, though he has a certain pity for the isolated and the dim. Social corruption is his target and most of his characters are there for our contempt, or to teach us self-contempt. Newby merely wants us to know ourselves, not to despise ourselves. In believing that the individual self, quite apart from the public life, quite outside vulgar social success or failure—the self as the soul—matters very much, Newby is perhaps unique among contemporary British novelists.

II. THE EARLIER NOVELS

Newby, then, is extremely productive. He depends, more than most novelists of his stature, on very skilful plot construction. His subject is the psyche rather than the polis: the intimate and hidden self rather than the outer network of society. In his plotting, he appears to remember Aristotle's *Poetics*. He uses the device of irony (the hero, like King Oedipus, understands how awful his situation is, but he persuades himself to the very last that it is the situation of somebody else). He uses the Aristotelian device at the end of the story of discovery or recognition, with its accompanying emotions (for hero and audience) of a sense of inevitability and a sense of unbearable shock. Strangely, however, unless one takes the crude test of the death of the hero at the end, he does not seem to me ever to have written a proper tragedy. *Something to Answer For* and *Agents and Witnesses* might be called passion plays. Most of the other novels are light or very serious comedies, in which there may be much suffering, but there is redemption at the end. There is one pure farce, *One of the Founders*, and there are novels, not verging on tragedy, but showing that crime does not pay, such as *The Barbary Light*, which might be described as morality plays.

I shall analyse Newby's first two novels, *Journey to the Interior* and *Agents and Witnesses* in great detail, for the first is a magnificent success, the second a magnificent failure. Like many a young man's early novels they carry the implications of what Newby was to do later and perhaps the promise of something he never quite did do. They have a hallucinatory and poetic quality which, achieving in compensation other qualities, he was never quite to recreate again (any more than one can recreate one's youth). Newby's novels seem to me to sort themselves out in three blocks: early romanticism: comedy: and compassionate realism. Detailed plot analysis for each novel in each block would be impossible. But I shall analyse *some* of the novels in a reasonably detailed way, not always those I necessarily think the best novels of a particular period, but sometimes those which I think most representative of certain weaknesses as well as strengths.

Newby's first novel, *A Journey to the Interior* (1945), is about grief, about how it seems to stop the heart and the clock, and yet about how, if we have the courage to explore the interior desert of the heart, we may, however much 'possessed by death', dowse the springs of life again. The name of the hero, Winter, is itself an allegory. He has lost his wife in childbirth, and the child was stillborn. He is sent by his firm, at once to convalesce and to keep an eye on things, to the remote Sultanate of Rasuka. Rasuka, like ancient Gaul, is divided into three parts. There is the port and city where the Sultan's writ runs. There is the station or compound where the company's writ runs. And there is the desert where the sword's writ runs: rival petty chiefs are always feuding and explorers do not return alive. On Rasuka, Winter's firm produces, unprofitably, five hundred barrels of oil a year, but it is worth their while to keep a foothold in the Sultanate.

The theme of the ambiguous power of death over the heart is firmly stated in the first chapter. Winter, voyaging to Rasuka on an Arab steamship, is disturbed by the wailings of the woman in the next cabin. Her husband has died in the night. But is her weeping sincere, or self-indulgent, or a thing of custom? She may have poisoned her elderly husband; but yet her weeping may still be sincere. Set ashore, Winter is confronted with other parables. He is greeted almost too effusively by his company's local manager, Mr Ford. Ford is ebullient, childish. His great pride is a cotton-winding machine which he claims to have worked out from first principles himself. The local doctor says it is all a cheat, copied from blue prints sent from London. Ford's wife is hostile to Winter, devoured by unsatisfied sexuality. Ford is clearly a weak man. He avoids trouble, and there is trouble; Hebechi, the native assistant to the unpleasant accountant, Cator, is suspected of having embezzled a hundred pounds. Ford does not want to sack Hebechi, but neither does he want to examine Cator's books when the suggestion is made that Hebechi is Cator's scapegoat. Only quite late in the story does Winter realize that Ford is not only weak and over-excitable but certifiably mad. Ford depends entirely on the protection provided by his wife: she treats him contemptuously, like a half-witted child, but does protect him devotedly.

The Sultan warns Winter not to explore the desert interior. An eccentric Englishman, Rider, has recently disappeared in the desert, almost certainly murdered. The Sultan makes a strangely mixed impression on Winter. He has a kind of childishly prurient curiosity about the sex lives of the unmarried Europeans in the Compound. He is exquisitely courteous, and yet his face is that of a man sensual, callous, and amoral. Yet at the same time there is a kind of unashamed human completeness in the Sultan. Winter, whose own life is in fragments, envies this quality. Winter also begins to build up a romantic picture of Rider. Rider was a feckless man, distributing drugs from the Company's dispensary not only to the Company's servants but to anyone who asked for them. This wasteful generosity, depleting stocks, led in the end to a riot, bloodily dispersed by the Sultan's soldiery. Was Rider really romantic? He was dirty and untidy, and two white women on the compound to whom he had made advances had treated him as a joke. Perhaps, like Ford, he was mad. Certainly, like Winter, he was a solitary, and Winter feels an odd urge to recapitulate Rider's experiences. Yet no one had really respected or loved Rider. His foolish generosity with drugs made no impression on the natives. Winter sees Rider's house burning down and the native crowd making no attempt to put the fire out, but taking great risks to loot the furniture.

Winter thinks that, with his wife's death, his sexual impulses are dead. But visiting his only previous acquaintance on the Compound, an Irish engineer called Flynn, he is startled, deceived by an effect of sunlight, by the apparition of his dead wife. The resemblance is not very close. The woman, Cator's secretary Nellie, has been sitting unnaturally still because Flynn is painting her portrait. Winter and Nellie become lovers, but Nellie is resentfully aware that Winter is making love to his dead wife's ghost. Winter's sexual obsession with the image of a dead woman makes him exciting even to Mrs Ford, who dislikes him very much as a person:

> Between them, this rather coarse woman and himself, Winter felt that almost anything was possible. Ford himself was too much of a fool to be angry with. But his wife had sensuality and a wish to disgust herself. *Winter, like all men, had this wish.*[1] He felt that he could love this woman with the greatest brutality. The situation between them was electric. When he was in a room with her the only thing he could think of was sex. (ch. viii).

The sentence italicized, and indeed the whole paragraph, display a disabused realism about sex, which is French rather than English, and remarkable in so young a man. Newby was twenty-seven when he published this novel and probably about twenty-five when he began to think it out. The italicized sentence also illustrates one of Newby's points about the good novel. It forces one to ask uncomfortable questions about *oneself.*

Hebechi, the Arab accused of forgery, sends a hysterical summons to Winter to meet him in the open air. Winter, who now has his own quarters, and is reluctantly giving a house-warming party for his fellow Europeans, ignores the message. Unfortunately Cator, who is Hebechi's accuser, arrives late at the party and on his way Hebechi makes a futile attempt to murder him. The Sultan, always placatory, wonders if Winter would like Hebechi tortured before he is

[1] My italics.

hanged. But the distressed Winter makes it clear that this is not what he wants at all and, probably with the Sultan's connivance, Hebechi escapes with suspicious ease from his cell. He flees to the desert and, with the Sultan's very reluctant permission, Winter pursues him attended by camels and three guards, whom he has to pay for himself. With one of these guards—a young soldier, gay, handsome, boastful, a liar—Winter, though not with any sexual consciousness, half falls in love. The boy thaws something in him. It is the boy, of course, who is killed in an ambush. He is solemnly buried. Winter turns back towards the City and the Compound. Some rite of placation has been performed and Winter is no longer really interested in discovering either Hebechi or Rider. Winter dismisses his two other attendants (who at various times on the trek have been thinking of assassinating him) on the outskirts of the Compound. He learns that after his departure poor Ford has gone quite mad and smashed up his precious toy, the home-made cotton-winding machine. Winter feels no emotion about this or about the pain he is about to inflict on his old friend Flynn, who loves Nellie. But Winter himself now loves Nellie, as herself, not as the enfleshed phantom of his dead wife. He asks her to marry him, she accepts, the frozen past at last completely thaws, the future comes alive. Spring has come, cruelly, and the dead will bury their dead. This is a strange hallucinatory novel, but on the last page everything suddenly makes retrospective sense, a closed fan suddenly flicking open.

Second novels are often disappointing. *Agents and Witnesses* (1947) has the same hallucinatory vividness, the same dream logic as *A Journey to the Interior*, but there is something arbitrary, both about its plot and about the motives of its characters. The setting is again imaginary—this time a Mediterranean island—but there are obvious echoes of Egypt, a corrupt cosmopolitan capital, rather like Cairo, and an interior where peasants, thought of as men of another race, are ruthlessly exploited and die like flies from endemic malaria.

The hero, a young French architect called Pierre, is rather like Camus's Meursault in *L'Étranger*, incapable of normal human responses, of warm love or poignant grief, but unlike Meursault, uneasily aware of his own shallowness. Pierre gets mixed up with Sourelli Pasha, a retired but very rich and influential politician. It is a whim, or perhaps a touch of remaining virtue, in Sourelli that he cares about the peasantry and finances a doctor who is trying to eradicate the malaria mosquito. But it is Sourelli's vice or weakness that he cannot refuse anything to his ruthless and amoral son, Nabil, who is plotting a *coup d'état* to put his father nominally in power and then take over full power himself.

Without a doubt there are echoes here of what Cairo must have been like in the time of Nahas Pasha and the uneasy later days of King Farouk. The imaginary island is a discreet disguise (Newby must have begun to write the novel before he left Egypt in 1946). Pierre is having a hesitant affair with a girl called Anna Keats, whose sister Marthe hates him for his unkindness to Anna, and who is herself Nabil's tool and lover. Sourelli sends Pierre to the malaria-stricken interior. Pierre is a physical coward as well as a tepid lover. Dr Pegia, the malaria expert, wants to see Sourelli Pasha, and Pierre eagerly offers to drive him back to the capital, so that he himself can escape from the risk of malaria. In a motor accident, Pegia is killed. Even Pierre's shallow heart is moved by Pegia's last words: 'A man has to create something in order to have a right to live.'

Pierre is also moved by the strange innocence, almost supernatural and transparent, of a little waitress at the inn where he lodges. He calls her Second Person for, in her imperfect French, she uses the pronoun *tu* for all French pronouns. The episode made me wonder whether Newby had been reading Martin Buber's *I and Thou*, a great mystical treatise translated into English by Ronald McGregor Smith in 1937. Pierre has to revisit the interior again and the news that Second Person is dead desolates him. The words of a monk who attempts to console him fill Pierre not with love but with rage and hate: yet even that is a kind of spiritual awakening. He rushes back to the capital, to see Anna again, and to throw in his lot with Nabil. He does see Anna, who rushes into the rioting streets after him. But from the windows of a local newspaper office, which his strong-arm men have seized, Nabil, egged on by Marthe, picks off Pierre with a rifle. Anna will find only a dead body sprawled on the pavement . . .

This summary perhaps suggests a touch of melodrama and more than a touch of the arbitrary in the story. Yet there are things that linger in the memory: Pierre's awareness of his own spiritual aridity: the childlike remote saintliness of Second Person: Anna's persistent loving of a man who has persistently confessed to her the hollowness of his own heart. Yet *Agents and Witnesses*, as some early reviewers suggested, makes gestures suggesting a significance that it never quite achieves. In its failed grand ambition, nevertheless, it does achieve a more striking memorability than most of the novels, deliberately more limited in their aims, which immediately succeed it. The Conrad of *Nostromo* could have handled Nabil's *coup d'état*, which, if one compares it with the actual *coup d'état* of Neguib and Nasser, a few years later, is quite singularly politically implausible. An effective *coup d'état*, in the Middle East and elsewhere, will be led by frugal, incorruptible soldiers, with a code of discipline, and probably from the educated lower middle classes; not by rich and irresponsible playboys like Nabil. Similarly, the theme of Pierre's spiritual aridity, and his spiritual awakening through grief and hate, required, if not a Dostoevsky, at least a Mauriac or a Bernanos. Yet one or two minor scenes and characters, particularly the scenes involving Second Person and Pierre's grief for her, are profoundly and permanently moving. *Agents and Witnesses* is like a young man's imperfect sketch for a great romantic novel which the more mature Newby was never able to write. As Newby developed, his sense of comedy, and of the psychological interest of quiet lives, gradually took over from his early taste for romance and mystery. His pleasure in tidy plotting (*Agents and Witnesses* presents no rational motivations) tended to make some of his later characters too neat, conventional, and flat. The subdued colours and weathers of the English landscape lent themselves, at first, to less effective descriptive writing than the hot, glaring contrasts of the Near East.

The next novel, *Mariner Dances* (1948), the first with an English setting, has something of this flatness and conventionality but, unlike *Agents and Witnesses*, is structurally perfect. And one character, Mariner, like a circus clown jumping through a burning hoop, upsets, and makes more real, the sedateness of the rest of the tale. There are two interlinked stories, in one of which the narrator, Fred Paul, is mainly spectator, in the other actor. As spectator Fred is intelligent, as actor confused. As a boy he had accidentally wounded his sister Gladys with a shotgun. She is pretty but permanently crippled and in frequent pain. Fred is a schoolmaster and takes one of his colleagues home as a possible husband for Gladys. The chosen suitor makes his own and different choice and brings his new fiancée to see the Pauls. In a mad fury, Paul beats the man up in the senior common room. But as a spectator Paul is helpful. A former colleague, Mariner, a man on the edge of insanity, all emotion and no character, has abducted a girl called Mary from her guardians without confessing that he already has a wife in Paris—the time is pre-World War II. Gladys and Mary run away together, Mary consents to marry Mariner, after he has divorced his wife, and on condition that she, not he, is boss. Mary has lost all illusions about Mariner but wants to keep her word. Fred, in his turn, realizes that his obsession with getting Gladys married springs not only from a sense of guilt about his boyish wounding of her, but also from a peculiar protective closeness between them which will, probably, make it as impossible for him as for Gladys to marry.

Mariner, though the most strangely vivid character in this novel, is also the most superficially implausible. Newby's old friend, the novelist Ernest Frost, tells me that both Mariner and a very similar character, Hesketh, who occurs in two later novels, *A Step to Silence* and *The Retreat*, were drawn from an actual eccentric whom Newby knew before the war in his training college and early teaching days. Mariner has the frightening unpredictability of life, and, set against him, the other characters, Mary, Gladys, Fred's wise old mother, his old father gruffly and with bewilderment facing the prospect of death, down to minor people, like

Mrs Hutton, Fred's gossipy landlady, all seem rather 'typical'. We have met them in a dozen other novels. Fred Paul is rounder, of course, since he has to have some of Newby's own subtlety of observation. But the novel is also a new kind of novel, comedy verging ominously on tragedy. When, in *The Retreat*, we see the last of Mariner's double, Hesketh, Hesketh is about to kill himself to save Fred's double, Oliver Knight, from a possible charge of murder and, at the least, from scandal and disgrace. In the mad, for Newby, there is a childish destructive egotism but also a potential heroism.

The next novel, *The Snow Pasture* (1949), set mainly in a Welsh mining village, is memorable mainly for its insight in describing the friendship between Benjy Pindar, the son of the local doctor, and Clem Johns, the son of the local ne'er-do-well: the grown-ups are not so interesting. The Second World War is over. It has left Dr Pindar without a sense of purpose; he has taken over the Welsh practice without any particular care for the village as a place, or for the people in it, and his emotional numbness puts a barrier between himself and both his son and his wife. Life comes back to the Pindar household when the tough young Clem Johns decides to settle in with them, and his rogue of a father tries to blackmail Pindar. Pindar intends to fight Johns but, over a drink, finds—with one of these touches of the unexpected that Newby can always use to revive a story that seems to be moving along too mechanically—that he rather likes the scoundrel. Benjy threatens his father, seriously, with a gun which the two boys have hidden away as a treasure, and Johns decides to 'take charge of his own kid'. Benjy Pindar is thought to have run away. Dr Pindar's numbness is melted by the return of his son and by the news that Mrs Pindar is again pregnant. There is a sub-plot about money. A summary like this suggests one danger to which Newby's steady productivity exposes him—that of turning out mere run-of-the-mill material. But in reading, *The Snow Pasture* is saved by a delicacy of natural description, rather like a faded water-colour, and by the vitality of the scenes with the boys, which counterpoint the tortuously introverted and emotionally constipated scenes with the adults.

There is nothing of this graceful, faded quality (and nothing of this over-refinement in handling adult emotion) in the next novel, *The Young May Moon* (1950). Here Newby develops, with a surer hand, the gift of getting inside a boy's mind, of which *The Snow Pasture* gave the first glimpses. But the grown-up characters have more colour, too: Uncle Adrian, the fatuously philosophizing baker, who swigs away at whisky bottles carefully hidden for him among the flour by his wife, has a near-Dickensian farcical breadth. Adrian is looking after his nephew Philip, whose stepmother (whom Philip thinks his real mother) has just died. Philip's real mother was a village beauty, loved by Philip's father Alec, by Adrian, and by Grainger, a successful hydraulic engineer for whom Laura left Alec shortly after Philip's birth. Philip's stepmother was a severe, stern woman who kept the feckless Alec in order. Yet Philip loved her. The happy widower dumps Philip on Adrian, to learn bakery, and wanders off in search of amorous adventures. The plot neatly brings Philip, Adrian, Alec, and Grainger together. There might be a fight but Laura is dead. Laura was 'something special', beyond good and evil, and the three men are at peace. Young Philip has meanwhile been feeling the first stirrings of adolescent sexuality, and hating them and also hating Laura. But through the grief of the three men who loved Laura, he reluctantly recognizes the power of beauty, and how it transcends moral judgements. He begs the second Mrs Rice, the hard woman whom only he loved, in whatever heavenly mansion she may be, to forgive Laura. The feckless Alec now recognizes his responsibility to his son and that he must not marry Doll, the barmaid whom he has picked up, and who is as shallow as himself. Grainger in time will take on Philip (whose likeness to Laura he has recognized on first meeting him) as an apprentice engineer. This is a satisfactory novel all through, as *The Snow Pasture* is not. If Adrian is a fine figure of Dickensian farce, Philip, both as a character and a focus of consciousness, might remind us of the young Pip or the young David Copperfield. The delicacies of a father-son relationship (especially with an amiable but inadequate father) and the growing-pains of adolescent consciousness are excellently done.

The next three novels, *A Season in England* (1951), *A Step to Silence* (1952), and *The Retreat* (1953) all mark, though not dramatically, a steady progress in Newby's art. They handle tense and unpredictable situations with a new assurance. Two of them might be described as unhappy comedies; one, *The Retreat*, as a redemptive near-tragedy. They display what Ernest Frost calls a Rilkean characteristic in Newby, a tendency to approach his central theme of love contrapuntally through the themes of loss, frustration and death. Each novel also shows the obsession of this very orderly and well-organized man with his opposite, the unpredictable, impulsive, amoral, irresponsible person, who is, like Mariner or Hesketh, all emotion and no character.

One remarkable feature of *A Season in England* is its vivid evocation of how, after years in Egypt with its simple passions, its heat and its toffee-like feeling of hard golden crispness, the beauty of the English landscape and the evasiveness of English character seem hazy and unreal. The hero, returning to England after many years, falls in love with England, but gives up the parents of the dead colleague who resembles him, and who, he hopes, might become substitute parents for himself, gives up his dead friend's maddeningly attractive but amoral and perverse Greek widow.

A Step to Silence and *The Retreat* are really one novel, and should be reprinted as such. Oliver Knight in the first novel is a bright young student at a Teacher Training College a year or two before the war. He is protected from ragging and bullying by a mature student, called Hesketh, who is generally accepted as a clown, but suffers from suicidal impulses, and a hysterical lack of self-confidence. He can also, though, in defence of Oliver, be frighteningly violent. Like Mariner with Fred Paul, he demands everything that he wants, a loan of money from Oliver, or the love of Oliver's friend Jane, with an irrational and effective frenzy. Jane agrees to marry him when he is standing on the parapet of a bridge, threatening to throw himself over. Like Mary, in *Mariner Dances*, she exerts authority. But Hesketh's madness is infectious. Oliver's reaction to the marriage is to join the RAF. In *The Retreat*, because of an accident in the Channel, Oliver, now an RAF officer due for hospitalization, is able to assume a false identity and track down Jane. Jane has borne a stillborn child, has left Hesketh, is suffering from heart trouble, and going slightly mad. Oliver has now married and really loves not Jane but Helen, his wife. In a hotel bedroom in Oxford, he is struggling with Jane, wishing to leave her, and she dies of a heart attack. Hesketh, who has been silently spying on them, enters the bedroom, tells Oliver to go away, writes a confession of murder and suicide, and takes poison. Oliver might now go quietly back to his unit but decides to give himself up. This draws the estranged Helen back to him. His last question to her before going off with the police is: 'Do you know what I mean by sanctuary?' He means self-sacrifice. These two novels, taken together, seem to me to display a firmer sense of moral pattern than Newby had so far achieved. The riddle of the madman protecting the almost excessively sane man and of the sane man, but with no rejection of Hesketh, insisting on taking his own punishment is a kind of riddle that recurs in Newby. It is a good riddle because it has no neat and definite answer. Madness is destructive; but mere sanity is not enough. Destructiveness and generosity can grow together, are not to be relied on, but make mere prudence look small. In most human dilemmas there is an apparently easy way out, but it is not the real way out.

III. THE MIDDLE AND LATER NOVELS

Though there are excellent touches of humour, and though there is sharp observation of scene and character, the earlier novels of Newby, exotic or pastoral, could be described as romantic. They appeal, perhaps, more to our powers of imaginative projection than to our knowledge of life. In the 1950s, Newby's characters become more rounded and individual, and his scenes more various. He deploys larger casts. The plotting, still neat, does not show its bones so much. Newby finds more space for the random happening, the queer event, which does not necessarily further the story, but gives an added density of atmosphere and richness of texture to the narrative. The handling of words becomes easier, more transparent. The dialogue in the later novels, for instance, makes the dialogue in the earlier novels sound slightly stilted. Just as he has lost his earlier preoccupation with patches of deliberate 'fine writing', so the mature Newby no longer presses his symbolic implications on the reader's attention too hard. These later novels are more widely known (some of the best of the earlier novels are out of print). It was my intention, therefore, to treat them in a much more summary way. But this has not always proved possible, particularly in the two great Anglo-Egyptian comedies, *The Picnic at Sakkara*, and *A Guest and His Going*. Theme, structure, and mood in these two novels are inextricably interfused. So I shall not be able to be quite as summary in this concluding section as I had hoped. But there *are* other late novels which can be treated more briefly. One difficulty in writing about Newby is that the plot, which for many good novelists—Trollope, say, in his political novels—is a kind of loose hold-all in which the same characters may perpetually recur, is for Newby his most important novelistic tool.

The Picnic at Sakkara (1955), *Revolution and Roses* (1957) and *A Guest and His Going* (1959) are comedies in a very particular Newbeian sense. They are often (particularly in their use of physical stage props—a pistol, a motor car, a blowpipe with a poisoned arrow—and in their explosive confrontations of infuriated and euphoric characters) more like farce than comedy. But in another sense they are more painful than conventional comedy (without ever being 'sick' or 'cruel' comedy). In *A Guest and His Going*, the gradual, decent drying up both of Edgar Perry's marriage and his career, though not of his vocation as a teacher, are presented with dry humour but are painful. An eccentric character called Hillingdon who slowly goes mad, attempts to kill the euphoric Egyptian Muawiya (who has borrowed and smashed up his car) with a blowpipe, and is carted away to an asylum, might come out of a Brian Rix farce[1]. Yet, at another level, the character of Hillingdon is a profoundly moving study of a man who has never had to work

[1] An immensely popular series of British commercial theatrical farces.

for his living, has an air of importance and significance, but no real purpose of any kind in life. These three Egyptian novels remind me of Eric Bentley's remark that farce and tragedy, with their use of menace, unpredictability, and sudden violence are two literary genres closer to each other than either is to polite comedy.

However, of these two novels (*Revolution and Roses* acts as a link between them, but is a much slighter work), one can say that the central theme is not at all the apparently 'topical' theme, the relationship between England and Egypt, but something much deeper, the difference between madness and sanity and, at a puzzling angle to that, the difference between false logic and true impulse. Of the two main characters, Muawiya, the Egyptian student, is maddening and apparently utterly irresponsible, but he is not mad: he seems to spread destruction in his wake, yet essentially he is a life-giver. His tutor, Edgar Perry, who both loves Muawiya and is exasparated by him, always aims at being moderate and consistent, and yet he is most truly himself when he acts out of an unreasoning impulse of loyalty to the charming but irresponsible Muawiya.

Yet Perry is a reasonable man, and it is his very reasonableness that makes some of his colleagues and patrons think *he* is mad. In *The Picnic at Sakkara*, after Muawiya has rescued him from violently demonstrating students, Perry goes to give a private lesson to a rich and cultivated Pasha and his wife, a Princess of the Egyptian Royal House. Their drawing-room makes a pleasant contrast to his brawling students, but, when he suggests that what the students need is decent hostels, the Pasha and the Princess freeze up, and think Perry slightly mad. Everybody knows that students live like pigs. Some students whom Perry visits in their squalid lodgings seem to agree. They don't want hostels. There would be discipline. What would they do about sex? Still they recognize Perry as a good sort and carry him on their shoulders into the street, with the result that he is immediately arrested as a subversive agitator. When he is released, he is invited by the students to a picnic near the Pyramids. Muawiya has been told off by the Moslem Brotherhood to assassinate Perry. In one of the corridors of the pyramids he makes a ludicrous effort at this, snatches the revolver from Perry, who had first snatched it from him, and claims he has rescued Perry from a suicide attempt. For his failure, Muawiya is beaten up by the Moslem Brotherhood and Perry is sacked for being either hopelessly unstable or a subversive. Yet when Muawiya joins Perry and his silly, pretty wife Mary, with a splendid picnic basket, on the train from Cairo, neither Perry nor Mary can be angry with him.

Some years have passed between *The Picnic at Sakkara* and *A Guest and His Going*. The revolution has succeeded, Nasser is in power. Muawiya, as a former leading student revolutionary, is invited by the British Council to visit England. But he is living in the past and wishes to court martyrdom. A little confused by whisky, he drives Hillingdon's car away from a party, smashes it up, and takes refuge in the Egyptian Embassy, where he is just a nuisance. He escapes from the Embassy and makes a passionate anti-British speech at a public debating society. Nobody is in the least annoyed. He thinks of making a speech in Hyde Park, but realizes that Speakers' Corner is a joke. Finally, he climbs by a window into Perry's language school and is hit with a harmless dart from Hillingdon's blowpipe. Confined to an asylum, Hillingdon cannot give evidence, the case is dismissed, and both the Egyptian Embassy and the British Council simply want to send Muawiya home. Perry has his own troubles: an unloving wife, middle age, a dull job which he must endure at the Helvetia Language School. Perry's life once meant something other than mere duty. Muawiya and his kind meant something in the early days of Egyptian independence, but now he is simply a nuisance to the professionals, like the Egyptian military attaché in London, Captain Yehia. Yet neither Perry nor Muawiya has relapsed into the sourness that has staled Perry's wife Mary or his former boss (now his assistant) Waldo Grimbley. In Egypt, Waldo was a mechanically sentimental pro-Arabist; in London, sacked from his Egyptian professorship, he is a mechanically rancorous anti-Arabist. Mary had expected Perry's career to be more glamorous and successful, and in his shabby London language school, with neither academic nor social glamour, she is bored. Besides, he is developing a paunch; and she is beginning to feel that sex is neither so important nor attractive as it is made out to be. Yet as we follow Perry and Muawiya in their long farewell walk round the squares and churches and palaces of London, we feel that, though neither was made for permanent success, each has achieved something more important, authenticity, and generosity of heart. *The Picnic at Sakkara* is a golden comedy with perhaps the last of Newby's youth in it; traversing disasters, it ends on an upswing. *A Guest and His Going*, more overtly farcical in its machinery, is rich but autumnal. Saying farewell to Muawiya, Perry is saying farewell to youth; though there will be no Moslem Brotherhood to beat him up this time, Muawiya, back in Egypt, will grow older and melt into the crowd. His enthusiastic bungling will cease to charm in life but on the page it permanently charms us.

Again out of chronological order but as Newby's last book with a fully Egyptian setting, we could take *Something to Answer For* (1968), set in the year of the Suez crisis, though written ten years later. It has something of the vivid colour, violence, and mysteriousness of Newby's first two novels, *Journey to the Interior* and *Agents and Witnesses*. It has something also of their hallucinatory quality. Briefly, the hero is a minor crook who has been treated kindly, when he was stationed as a sergeant in Suez, by a rich merchant and his wife. He has been helping himself to a trust fund which he controls (the beneficiaries are hard to find), is guilty and at a loose end, and wants to get out of England. The benevolent merchant is dead, and he dallies with the idea of either marrying the widow or becoming her man of business. But his purposes are slowly undermined. On the way out, he is insulted by a Jew who says the British are even more responsible than the Germans for Hitler's massacres. They could have warned the Jews. In Suez, he visits what used to be his favourite pub, and outside it is beaten up and stripped naked. In the end, far from exploiting the widow, he has to risk his life getting her on a ship to America, and has to flee from Suez in a small boat with only a tin of bully beef and no tin-opener. The waves beat on his boat and will probably swamp it. But he faces death with an odd exultation. He has 'something to answer for'. I know readers who rank this among Newby's finest novels. To me, his Augustinian obsession with the notion of the human need for self-punishment, of atonement through arbitrary seeking out of suffering, morally unbalances the book: the Jansenist tradition becomes too like masochism.

A more balanced though less exciting book on the same sort of 'morality play' theme is *The Barbary Light* (1962). As a boy, Owen Hanner had boarded a ship in South Wales with the romantic hope of sailing to the Barbary coast. The sailors pretend to humour him but land him back at Cardiff pier. Thereafter, in a quiet way, he decides to create his own Barbary coast for himself. His wife Sybil lives in the country, but in London he has a mistress, Alex, who does not know that he is married. He is an accountant concerned with bankruptcy cases and uses his knowledge to make money on the side. A man threatened with bankruptcy will often have to sell cheaply a factory site or land suitable for development, and Hanner can expect a good rake-off from potential buyers. The plot is rather predictable. Sybil discovers Alex ill in Owen's London flat and both women return to the country, and become equally inaccessible to Owen. An angry bankrupt gives away the secret about Owen's rake-offs and he has to face a Disciplinary Court. He does so, losing his professional status, but Sybil is now ready to take him back and Alex to fade away. Owen will settle in future for Cardiff pier. It is a very moral but rather smug story and reminds one of Newby's admiration for that most moralistic of British novelists, Maria Edgeworth. Belated virtue has to be very much its own reward, and crime certainly does not pay.

One might mention here in passing Newby's one volume of short stories, *Ten Miles from Anywhere* (1958). It is dissatisfying in the same way as *The Barbary Light*: here is a craftsman working perfectly within his limits, but all too safely within them. The two stories I remember best are 'Uncle Kevork', which combines the humour of the *Arabian Nights* with that of Damon Runyon, and 'The Heat of Texas'. The latter shows a coolly intimate understanding of brutality and, as it returns to one's mind at uninvited moments, one half wishes one had not read it. But the stories as a group are good spare-time exercises and Newby would not claim to be a short story writer of the order of Joyce, Kipling, Lawrence, or Katherine Mansfield. The short stories, like *The Barbary Light* and like some of the earlier novels with an English setting, indicate a paradoxical weakness or flaw in Newby's equipment and achievement. He is so thoroughly a professional, can do in such a finished way whatever he sets out to do, that he does not often enough risk stretching himself to, and beyond, his limits.

But this criticism does not apply to the last two novels to be dealt with in this essay, *One of the Founders* (1965) and *A Lot to Ask* (1973). *One of the Founders*, light and frothy, but beautifully whipped up, is Newby's one exercise in pure light comedy. *A Lot to Ask*, a wholly serious novel, returns to a theme which is almost an obsession with Newby, that of madness, but we see Arthur Poumphrey not, as we see Hesketh or Mariner, from the outside. We see Poumphrey's world from inside Poumphrey's own head, the head of an impulsive extrovert, who has made himself rich and famous by following irrational hunches, which generally work out successfully. Poumphrey himself feels that something odd is happening to his mind. He meets, for instance, a Foreign Office official on a plane and, introduced to someone of the same name at a restaurant, he thinks that the man looks quite different. He gets a series of threatening telephone calls warning him not to visit the Middle East. Is it a serious warning, a hoax, possibly a hallucination? He goes to the Middle East to look up an old friend in an official post, who hysterically denies all knowledge of him; later, it seems that, because of Poumphrey's visit, the man has been executed. The company of which he is chairman becomes more and more alarmed not so much about his 'sanity' as about his 'soundness'. Deprived of his chairmanship, he takes up politics, but fails to be adopted as a candidate for a vacant seat. It adds to his worries that he has never known his mother, who left his father when he was young. He finds a mysterious old lady in Cornwall who, teasingly, will not confess whether she is his mother or not. He decides to cuckold his successful rival for the candidature but on the same night to go and spy on the old lady, who has been joined by Poumphrey's long-suffering wife. Getting back to London, to the candidate's wife's flat, he passes in the hall someone uncannily like himself, and the lady, when he goes back to bed, incapable of making love, seems to think that he has been in the house all night. Has the journey to Cornwall been a hallucination, or is the lady hoaxing him, and has she been in bed with another lover?

Instead of blowing up, however, Poumphrey unexpectedly winds down. He realizes that he is ill in some mysterious way and goes off with his wife, the only woman whom he has ever really loved, to convalesce and laze. People now remember that he was maddening, but had luck. He could have a career in politics; his firm might take him back. He is benignly uninterested. The strange old lady in Cornwall, mother-figure if not mother, has acted as a kind of white witch. The idea of male aggressiveness has ceased to be fun. Newby here *has* stretched himself, writing a comedy of madness and healing from the patient's point of view. One should insist that the book *is* a comedy: we are very concerned about Arthur Poumphrey but he is also, unconsciously, very funny. We are left also, though Newby never deals directly with political themes, with the uncomfortable thought that a combination of paranoia, megalomania, and hypertension may, in fact, in our world as it is today, characterize a high proportion of our most respected leaders.

Yet Newby's final message to his readers is not exactly 'It's a mad world, my masters'. The madness, the unpredictability and oddity, is, up to a certain intuitively definable limit, what makes life full of relish for him. He enjoys an Arabian Nights rogue or a Dickensian obsessive. His attitude even towards those of his characters who could be called definitely mean or evil is one of sad sympathy rather than cold condemnation. But with this tolerance there goes rigour. Life is very precarious. There are illusions which are attractive but in the end destructive. There are risks which, in honour, one has to take, but taking them may prove fatal. There are hopes, as in Oliver Knight's or Edgar Perry's cases, that are real and fresh in youth but that are subtly thwarted or withered as one grows older. Much in life depends on having the right intuition, and the tact to go with the intuition, at the right moment: but we can have no guarantee that this will happen. The final picture of life that emerges for me from Newby's novels is that of life as rich, funny, but terrifyingly uncertain. There are traps everywhere. Caught in a trap, one can still preserve a certain integrity. 'Religious' is an adjective of very wide and vague connotations, especially today, but I would describe Newby, in his feelings, not in any doctrines he may believe, as a religious novelist in the Protestant rather than the Catholic tradition. In the Catholic tradition, an institution, the Church, may absolve one of one's sins. In the extreme late Protestant tradition one is forced, like so many of Newby's characters, to judge oneself: and strangely one can often, like the hero of *Something to Answer For*, reach self-forgiveness only through self-condemnation.

P. H. NEWBY

A Select Bibliography

(Place of publication London, unless otherwise stated)

Separate Works:

A JOURNEY TO THE INTERIOR (1945). *Novel*
AGENTS AND WITNESSES: A Novel (1947).
THE SPIRIT OF JEM (1947). *Children's Fiction*
—with illustrations by Keith Vaughan.
MARINER DANCES (1948). *Novel*
THE SNOW PASTURE (1949). *Novel*
THE LOOT RUNNERS (1949). *Children's Fiction*
—with illustrations by F. Stock May.
THE YOUNG MAY MOON (1950). *Novel*
MARIA EDGEWORTH (1950)
—'English Novelists' series.
A PLAIN AND LITERAL TRANSLATION OF THE ARABIAN NIGHTS' ENTERTAINMENTS, by Sir Richard Burton: A Selection by P. H. Newby (1950)
—twelve stories from this selection were further reprinted in 1960.
A SEASON IN ENGLAND: A Novel (1951).
THE NOVEL, 1945–1950 (1951). *Criticism*
—a British Council pamphlet in the 'Arts in Britain' series.
A STEP TO SILENCE (1952). *Novel*
THE RETREAT (1953). *Novel.*
THE PICNIC AT SAKKARA (1955). *Novel*
REVOLUTION AND ROSES (1957). *Novel*
TEN MILES FROM ANYWHERE & OTHER STORIES (1958).
A GUEST AND HIS GOING: A Novel (1959).
THE BARBARY LIGHT (1962). *Novel*
ONE OF THE FOUNDERS (1965). *Novel*
SOMETHING TO ANSWER FOR (1968). *Novel*
A LOT TO ASK (1973). *Novel*

Biographical and Critical Studies:

General:

'P. H. Newby', by V. Colby, *Wilson Library Bulletin*, March 1953.
'Newby: Experience as farce', by H. H. Watts, *Perspective* (St Louis), X, 1958.

'Portrait of the artist as a Jung man', by L. Dickerson, *Kenyon Review*, XXI, 1959
—examines the use of Jungian concepts in Newby's novels.
'A Novelist on his own', *Times Literary Supplement*, 6 April 1962.
A READER'S GUIDE TO THE CONTEMPORARY ENGLISH NOVEL, by F. R. Karl (1963)
—first published in New York as *The Contemporary English Novel*, 1962. Includes a section 'A Search for P. H. Newby' in the chapter entitled 'The Novel as moral allegory: The fiction of William Golding, Iris Murdoch, Rex Warner and P. H. Newby'.
'Quest in the novels of P. H. Newby', by E. F. Bufkin, *Criticism*, VIII, Fall 1965.
'Newby on the Nile: The Comic Trilogy', by F. X. Mathews, *Twentieth Century Literature*, XIV, April 1968.
'Something to celebrate', by T. Coleman, *The Guardian*, 23 April 1969.
'First Booker Fiction Prize awarded to P. H. Newby for *Something to Answer for*', *The Bookseller*, 26 April 1969.
'Witness to violence: The War novels of P. H. Newby', by F. X. Mathews, *Texas Studies in Literature and Language*, XII, 1970.
'Manners and myths in the novels of P. H. Newby', by S. Poss, *Critique: Studies in Modern Fiction*, XII, i, 1970.

Selected Reviews:

A JOURNEY TO THE INTERIOR
J. Strachey. *Horizon*, May 1946.

THE SPIRIT OF JEM
J. Stern. *New York Times Book Review*, 10 September 1967.
Times Literary Supplement, 30 November 1967.

MARIA EDGEWORTH
L. de la Torre. *New York Times Book Review*, 6 August 1950.
Nineteenth-Century Fiction, V, 1950.
Notes and Queries, CXCV, 1950.
Times Literary Supplement, 28 April 1950.

THE RETREAT
P. Pickrel. *Yale Review*, Summer 1963.

THE PICNIC AT SAKKARA
I. Quigly. *The Spectator*, 15 April 1955.
H. Corke. *The Listener*, 28 April 1955.
J. Stern. *Encounter*, May 1955.
M. Richardson. *New Statesman & Nation*, 14 May 1955.

J. K. Hutchens. *New York Herald Tribune Book Review*, 28 August 1955.
C. Baker. *Nation*, 10 September 1955.

REVOLUTION AND ROSES
C. Baker. *Saturday Review*, 20 July 1957.
G. Weales. *Commonweal*, 9 August 1957.
D. Macdonald. *Encounter*, September 1957.

TEN MILES FROM ANYWHERE & OTHER STORIES
F. Wyndham. *London Magazine*, August 1958.

A GUEST AND HIS GOING
Times Literary Supplement, 19 June 1959.
V. S. Naipaul. *New Statesman*, 20 June 1959.
R. Gutwilling. *Commonweal*, 15 January 1960.
J. Stern. *New York Times Book Review*, 17 January 1960.
F. T. Wood. *English Studies* (Amsterdam), October 1960.

THE BARBARY LIGHT
M. Richardson. *New Statesman*, 6 April 1962.
R. Bryden. *The Spectator*, 6 April 1962.
Times Literary Supplement, 6 April 1962.
V. Scannell. *The Listener*, 19 April 1962.

ONE OF THE FOUNDERS
J. Brooke. *The Listener*, 30 September 1965.
S. Wall. *London Magazine*, December 1965.
A. West. *New Yorker*, 25 December 1965.

SOMETHING TO ANSWER FOR
W. Hildick. *The Listener*, 14 November 1968.
M. Wilding. *London Magazine*, February 1969.
C. Ricks. *New York Review of Books*, 5 June 1969.
W. Sheed. *New Yorker*, 6 September 1969.

A LOT TO ASK
D. J. Enright. *The Listener*, 3 May 1973.
Times Literary Supplement, 11 May 1973.

WRITERS AND THEIR WORK

General Surveys:

THE DETECTIVE STORY IN BRITAIN: Julian Symons
THE ENGLISH BIBLE: Donald Coggan
ENGLISH VERSE EPIGRAM: G. Rostrevor Hamilton
ENGLISH HYMNS: Arthur Pollard
ENGLISH MARITIME WRITING: Hakluyt to Cook: Oliver Warner
THE ENGLISH SHORT STORY I: & II: T. O. Beachcroft
THE ENGLISH SONNET: P. Cruttwell
ENGLISH SERMONS: Arthur Pollard
ENGLISH TRANSLATORS AND TRANSLATIONS: J. M. Cohen
ENGLISH TRAVELLERS IN THE NEAR EAST: Robin Fedden
THREE WOMEN DIARISTS: M. Willy

Sixteenth Century and Earlier:

FRANCIS BACON: J. Max Patrick
BEAUMONT & FLETCHER: Ian Fletcher
CHAUCER: Nevill Coghill
GOWER & LYDGATE: Derek Pearsall
RICHARD HOOKER: Arthur Pollard
THOMAS KYD: Philip Edwards
LANGLAND: Nevill Coghill
LYLY & PEELE: G. K. Hunter
MALORY: M. C. Bradbrook
MARLOWE: Philip Henderson
SIR THOMAS MORE: E. E. Reynolds
RALEGH: Agnes Latham
SIDNEY: Kenneth Muir
SKELTON: Peter Green
SPENSER: Rosemary Freeman
THREE 14TH-CENTURY ENGLISH MYSTICS: Phyllis Hodgson
TWO SCOTS CHAUCERIANS: H. Harvey Wood
WYATT: Sergio Baldi

Seventeenth Century:

SIR THOMAS BROWNE: Peter Green
BUNYAN: Henri Talon
CAVALIER POETS: Robin Skelton
CONGREVE: Bonamy Dobrée
DONNE: F. Kermode
DRYDEN: Bonamy Dobrée
ENGLISH DIARISTS: Evelyn and Pepys: M. Willy
FARQUHAR: A. J. Farmer
JOHN FORD: Clifford Leech
GEORGE HERBERT: T. S. Eliot
HERRICK: John Press
HOBBES: T. E. Jessop
BEN JONSON: J. B. Bamborough
LOCKE: Maurice Cranston
ANDREW MARVELL: John Press
MILTON: E. M. W. Tillyard
RESTORATION COURT POETS: V. de S. Pinto
SHAKESPEARE: C. J. Sisson
CHRONICLES: Clifford Leech
EARLY COMEDIES: Derek Traversi
LATER COMEDIES: G. K. Hunter
FINAL PLAYS: F. Kermode
HISTORIES: L. C. Knights
POEMS: F. T. Prince
PROBLEM PLAYS: Peter Ure
ROMAN PLAYS: T. J. B. Spencer
GREAT TRAGEDIES: Kenneth Muir
THREE METAPHYSICAL POETS: Margaret Willy
WEBSTER: Ian Scott-Kilvert
WYCHERLEY: P. F. Vernon

Eighteenth Century:

BERKELEY: T. E. Jessop
BLAKE: Kathleen Raine
BOSWELL: P. A. W. Collins
BURKE: T. E. Utley
BURNS: David Daiches
WM COLLINS: Oswald Doughty
COWPER: N. Nicholson
CRABBE: R. L. Brett
DEFOE: J. R. Sutherland
FIELDING: John Butt
GAY: Oliver Warner
GIBBON: C. V. Wedgwood
GOLDSMITH: A. Norman Jeffares
GRAY: R. W. Ketton-Cremer
HUME: Montgomery Belgion

SAMUEL JOHNSON: S. C. Roberts
POPE: Ian Jack
RICHARDSON: R. F. Brissenden
SHERIDAN: W. A. Darlington
CHRISTOPHER SMART: G. Grigson
SMOLLETT: Laurence Brander
STEELE, ADDISON: A. R. Humphreys
STERNE: D. W. Jefferson
SWIFT: J. Middleton Murry
SIR JOHN VANBRUGH: Bernard Harris
HORACE WALPOLE: Hugh Honour

Nineteenth Century:
MATTHEW ARNOLD: Kenneth Allott
JANE AUSTEN: S. Townsend Warner
BAGEHOT: N. St John-Stevas
THE BRONTËS: I & II: Winifred Gérin
BROWNING: John Bryson
E. B. BROWNING: Alethea Hayter
SAMUEL BUTLER: G. D. H. Cole
BYRON: I, II & III: Bernard Blackstone
CARLYLE: David Gascoyne
LEWIS CARROLL: Derek Hudson
COLERIDGE: Kathleen Raine
CREEVEY & GREVILLE: J. Richardson
DE QUINCEY: Hugh Sykes Davies
DICKENS: K. J. Fielding
EARLY NOVELS: T. Blount
LATER NOVELS: B. Hardy
DISRAELI: Paul Bloomfield
GEORGE ELIOT: Lettice Cooper
FERRIER & GALT: W. M. Parker
FITZGERALD: Joanna Richardson
ELIZABETH GASKELL: Miriam Allott
GISSING: A. C. Ward
THOMAS HARDY: R. A. Scott-James and C. Day Lewis
HAZLITT: J. B. Priestley
HOOD: Laurence Brander
G. M. HOPKINS: Geoffrey Grigson
T. H. HUXLEY: William Irvine
KEATS: Edmund Blunden
LAMB: Edmund Blunden
LANDOR: G. Rostrevor Hamilton
EDWARD LEAR: Joanna Richardson
MACAULAY: G. R. Potter
MEREDITH: Phyllis Bartlett
JOHN STUART MILL: M. Cranston
WILLIAM MORRIS: P. Henderson
NEWMAN: J. M. Cameron
PATER: Ian Fletcher
PEACOCK: J. I. M. Stewart
ROSSETTI: Oswald Doughty
CHRISTINA ROSSETTI: G. Battiscombe
RUSKIN: Peter Quennell
SIR WALTER SCOTT: Ian Jack
SHELLEY: G. M. Matthews
SOUTHEY: Geoffrey Carnall
LESLIE STEPHEN: Phyllis Grosskurth
R. L. STEVENSON: G. B. Stern
SWINBURNE: Ian Fletcher
TENNYSON: B. C. Southam
THACKERAY: Laurence Brander
FRANCIS THOMPSON: P. Butter
TROLLOPE: Hugh Sykes Davies
OSCAR WILDE: James Laver
WORDSWORTH: Helen Darbishire

Twentieth Century:
CHINUA ACHEBE: A. Ravenscroft
JOHN ARDEN: Glenda Leeming
W. H. AUDEN: Richard Hoggart
SAMUEL BECKETT: J.-J. Mayoux
HILAIRE BELLOC: Renée Haynes
ARNOLD BENNETT: F. Swinnerton
EDMUND BLUNDEN: Alec M. Hardie
ROBERT BRIDGES: J. Sparrow
ANTHONY BURGESS: Carol M. Dix
ROY CAMPBELL: David Wright
JOYCE CAREY: Walter Allen
G. K. CHESTERTON: C. Hollis
WINSTON CHURCHILL: John Connell
R. G. COLLINGWOOD: E. W. F. Tomlin
I. COMPTON-BURNETT: R. Glynn Grylls
JOSEPH CONRAD: Oliver Warner
WALTER DE LA MARE: K. Hopkins
NORMAN DOUGLAS: Ian Greenlees
LAWRENCE DURRELL: G. S. Fraser
T. S. ELIOT: M. C. Bradbrook
T. S. ELIOT: The Making of 'The Waste Land': M. C. Bradbrook
FIRBANK & BETJEMAN: J. Brooke
FORD MADOX FORD: Kenneth Young
E. M. FORSTER: Rex Warner
CHRISTOPHER FRY: Derek Stanford